THE LIFE OF BERNADETTE

THE EARLY YEARS

Lourdes, 1844. A village in southwest France, Département of the High Pyrenees. Situated by the conjunction of seven vallys at the foot of the Pyrenees range just beneath a castle that once belonged to the Counts of Bigorre, it had a population of 4000, give or take a few.

The economy of the village was primarily based on the exploitation of marble and slate quarries and, of course, agriculture. Beyond the castle flowed the River Gave du Pau which, on the village outskirts, was joined by the Lapaca whose waters served to power the numerous mills along the way.

At 2:00 pm on January 7, 1844, in the humble Boly Mill on the banks of the Lapaca, a baby girl, Marie-Bernarde, was born to Louise Castérot and François Soubirous. Bernadette, as everyone called her and as she would later be known to the whole world, lived here for only a few months. When Bernadette was no more than an infant, her mother, then expecting another child, was badly burned in a fire sparked by a candle.

A maternal aunt, Bernarde, arranged to send the baby off to a wet nurse. The nurse, Marie Laguës Burg, resident of Bartrès, a town a couple of miles from Lourdes, had recently lost her eighteen-day-old son, and quickly grew exceedingly fond of the infant girl in her care. Bernadette stayed in Bartrès with the Burg family a full year, until April 1, 1846, when she was brought back to Boly. But other hardships lay in store for the Soubirous: in 1848 François lost his left eye when a stone chip flew into it as he was fixing one of his grindstones. Business got worse and worse, customers never paid on time, and financial troubles soon forced the family to move to another house, this one even more miserable than Boly.

Then, in 1854, they temporarily lived with the Laborde family and François accepted a job as a farmhand in a desperate attempt to support his family which had meanwhile doubled in size - Toinette, Jean-Marie, and Justin were born in those years.

In the fall of 1855 Bernadette came down with cholera during an epidemic which, in a few short months, took a toll of thirty victims in Lourdes. Her health, already undermined by the privations of her early years, was dealt another terrible blow, and, for the whole of her brief life, she bore the signs of the diseases that continued to plague her, not the least being asthma. But while disease was weakening Bernadette's body, it was at the same time tempering her soul. Yerars later she would say that she perceived the hardships she had gone through as trials that God was subjecting her to ("when you're sure that the dear Lord wishes it so, you don't complain.").

Other direct testimony bears out this side of her character — she was, according to witnesses, perpetually good-natured, never once complained, nor was she ever critical of anyone's behavior toward her.

Another year, another move. This time the Soubirous, hopeful of bettering their lot in life, moved to a mill in Arcizac-les-Angles, a couple of miles from Lourdes. The hope was shortlived. By the summer of 1856 the family was literally out on the street. François' cousin, André Sajous, took pity on his poor relatives, letting them move into an abandoned prison he owned. The family lodged in the most depressing section the so-called "Cachot" "an infected, gloomy hole" measuring 4 by 4½ yards.

In September 1857, Marie Laguës, who had nursed Bernadette eleven years before, asked her back to Bartrès. Bernadette would help with the house and farmwork and tend a flock of sheep. The only drawback was that she would have to give up the religious training she had started at Lourdes, for, despite the fact that she did not know how to read or write she was bent on taking her First Communion, and had learned prayers such as the Pater Nostrum, the Credo, and the Ave Maria by heart, an inexpensive set of rosary beads serving as her mass-book. Nevertheless, after a long day's toil, Bernadette would sit and study her Catechism, memorizing the proper responses. Then, in January 1858, she returned to the miserable Cachot on Rue des Petits Fossés and life went on as usual until February 11 of the very same year.

THE APPARITIONS

The First Apparition

February 11, 1858 fell on a melancholy rainy Thursday. There was no firewood at the Cachot, as the last bundle had been sold to procure a bit of food. Bernadette, her sister Toinette, and their friend Jeanne Abadie, nicknamed Baloume, volunteered to go down by the Gave and gather some wood. The three little girls started off towards the river, crossed the canal whose waters drove the Savy Mill, and went on until they reached the Isle of Chalet, a strip of land flanked on one side by the canal and on the other by the Gave as it curved beneath the castle precipice. Opposite the tongue of land where the canal and river met up loomed a huge rock overlying an elongated grotto about eight yards long; everyone called the spot Massabielle.

From their vantage point the children spied a nice pile of driftwood left by the Gave, but they would have to cross the stream to reach it. Bernadette, who was not too keen about wading into the ice cold water, hesitated a bit while the other girls

The Boly Mill. (Reconstruction by Musée du «Petit Lourdes»).

The Boly Mill today. ▶

were already on their way.

As Bernadette was well aware of her poor health and had been constantly told to be careful by her mother, she asked her companions to place some stepping stones in the water so she could avoid wetting her legs, but to no avail. There was no way out. She would have to take off her stockings, the little luxury which served as a bit of protection for her frail body.

Bernadette began undoing the first stocking. Later she would say that at this point she heard a strong gust of wind blowing but when she turned around, all was still and the trees weren't the slightest bit ruffled. She went back to undoing the stocking but when she heard the same noise again she raised her head and saw a woman standing in the grotto.

Bernadette described her as dressed in white with a white veil over her head, a skyblue girdle, and a rose on each foot. Clasped in her hands was a rosary of white beads. "Then I put my hand in my pocket and took out my rosary. I wanted to cross myself but I just couldn't get my hand up to my forehead, it was glued to my side", Bernadette recounted. When the Lady clad in white then raised the rosary and crossed herself, Bernadette managed to imitate her. At the end of this mystic recital of the Rosary, the Lady beckoned Bernadette to come towards her, but Bernadette was too frightened and the vision suddenly disappeard. This is how the first of Bernadette's many visions, eighteen all told, was described by the Maid of Lourdes herself.

When Bernadette caught up to the other girls, she couldn't resist asking them if they had seen anything. They replied that they hadn't but that they had noticed her acting a bit oddly. The question had evidently aroused their curiosity and on the whole trip home they begged her to confide in them. At long last, she broke down and confided in her sister Toinette alone, telling her briefly of the encounter in the grotto.

Toinette, however, couldn't keep a secret and reported everything to their mother who, frightened, hastened to question Bernadette. Her daughter's brief replies scared her even more — Bernadette was probably under the effect of a fever. She good-naturedly scolded the child and the next day, after conferring with cousin Sajous' wife, their upstairs neighbor, ended the matter by forbidding Bernadette ever to set foot in Massabielle again.

The Second Apparition

Sunday, February 14. Bernadette couldn't help feeling attracted to the grotto, despite her mother's adamant refusal to let her return. Her submissive nature prevented her from breaking the rules, but her longing was such that she got up enough courage to beg her mother's permission once more. This was not granted, so she turned to her father. The result would have been the same, had it not been for François Soubirous' employer M. Cazenave. What could be so terrible about a lady holding a rosary, he argued.

Having obtained her father's consent, Bernadette rushed off, accompanied by a group of friends, clasping a bottle of holy water taken from the local church in her hands. As soon as she arrived at the grotto, she started to recite the rosary. After only a short while the Lady appeared. Bernadette opened the bottle of holy water, and flung its contents in the Lady's direction. In Bernadette's words, "Then I started to throw holy water at her, saying that if she had been sent by God she should stay, otherwise she should leave. She smiled and bent her head. The more I sprinkled her, the more she smiled, bending down her head".

Bernadette's account stops here because, having fallen into the mystic ecstasy, she was unaware of what was going on around her. When she was speaking to the Lady in white, Baloume (annoyed at being left behind) pushed a large rock — "as big as a hat" — from the ledge above the grotto right into the midst of the group of girls gathered there.

5

The Church of Bartrès. (Reconstruction by Musée du «Petit Lourdes»).

Although nobody was hurt, the loud noise sparked general panic. The girls tried to drag Bernadette away, but her body suddenly seemed so heavy that their efforts were unsuccessful. Only Antoine Nicolau who heard the screams and came running from the nearby Savy Mill was able to get Bernadette out of the grotto. He too noticed how heavy her body was and how she kept her gaze riveted to the grotto throughout the whole trip to the mill.

Once they arrived at the mill, Bernadette came back to her senses. Summoned by the girls, her mother rushed to the village and Bernadette was almost given a sound beating. This was to be the last time, for, according to M. Soubirous, Bernadette would never again set foot in the grotto.

The Third Apparition

Thursday, February, 18. Bernadette went back to her normal life. Nonetheless, word had spread and she was bombarded with questions from the Sisters of Nevers, whose "free classes" she attended at the Hospice. The reactions she received consisted of mocking, rebukes, and commiseration, but she didn't react at all. Sorry that she had ever spoken, she decided to erect a wall of silence around herself.

One of the people who talked about the events of Massabielle was Mme. Milhet. Bernadette's description of the Lady's garments reminded her of the habit worn by the Daughters of Mary of Lourdes and she thought that maybe the figure was actually the ghost of a pious member of the group, Elisa Latapie, who had died prematurely just a few months before. Her curiosity was so great that Mme. Milhet did not hesitate to use her position as Louise Soubirous' sometime employer to wheedle permission for Bernadette to return to the grotto.

When the little group — Mme. Milhet, Bernadette and another lady, Mme. Peyret, who aided Mme. Milhet in her work as a seamstress — started out, day had not yet broken, for although Mme. Soubirous had consented, she waned to avoid any further publicity. Mme. Milhet had made up her mind that she would find out exaclty who the lady was and

what she wanted from the mysterious figure herself, and so she had brought pen, paper, and ink which Bernadette would hand over at the right moment. Also, for the first time, a candle was brought along. Shortly after they began clicking their rosary beads, the Lady appeared to Bernadette who, while in ecstasy, continued to recite her prayers. Then, pushed by the two women, Bernadette got up and stepped inside the grotto. As instructed, she requested the Lady, "if she had anything to tell her, to kindly write it down", as Bernadette later reported. "She smiled and said that what she had to say didn't require writing down, and she asked me if I would please come back for fifteen days".

Bernadette promised that she would. The Lady went on to say, "... I won't promise to make you happy in this world, but in the next one".

This was the first time the Lady had spoken.

The Fourth Apparition

Friday, February 19. At 6:00 am a dozen people including Bernadette's mother and aunt Bernarde, were present at Bernadette's meeting with the Lady who appeared after only three Ave Marias. Eyewitnesses observed that Bernadette's physical appearance underwent profound changes when she was in ecstasy — she became extremely pale, "waxlike", as they described her, and smiled with such tenderness that "it was a joy to behold her".

Bernadette never revealed anything about this encounter with the Lady she herself called "Aquerò". This name — actually dialect — has beeen widely discussed by scholars and is generally taken to mean "that one".

The Fifth Apparition

Saturday, February 20. News of the visions had begun to spread. That morning thirty-odd people were on hand to greet Bernadette when she arrived at Massabielle.

The Virgin appeared after a quarter of an hour of prayer although, at the end of the meeting, a veil of sadness had come over Ber-

Bartrès: interior of the Burg house.

nadette's face.

Bernadette would neither answer questions about the encounter nor reveal anything of what was said during the apparition. Nevertheless, on the basis of numerous reports, it is believed that the Virgin taught her a personal prayer.

The Sixth Apparition

Sunday, February 21. Bernadette asked her aunt Bernarde and uncle Basile to take her to the grotto early in the morning to avoid the presence of onlookers. Their plans were thwarted by the hundred or so people gathered to await her. This too was a "confidential" meeting, and nowhere, not even in her written reports, would she ever provide the details of the event.

The sixth apparition took place on a Sunday, the first day of Lent. Bernadette attended Mass and later the Vesper service. As she was leaving the church after Vespers, she was stopped by a policeman who brought her before Commissioner Jacomet for questioning. Jacomet, worried about the threat to law and order in the town and what his superiors would say, wanted to call a halt to these "rallies".

The meeting was held in the commissioner's home in front of which a growing crowd was calling loudly for Bernadette's release. Bernadette later recounted what had happened during the meeting and indeed an official transcription of it still exists. Jacomet attempted to make Bernadette admit embarassing things which she steadfastly refused to do. Jacomet's approach was to make comments that completely twisted the sense of her answers, and thus Bernadette would not sign the statement. In her words, "after having taken down a couple of line as I had dictated, he would throw in other things that I hadn't said. Then he told me he would read it aloud so I could see if he had made any mistakes. I listened carefully, and

The Cachot.

had to attend afternoon classes, right to the school grounds. Bernadette, who was plagued by the thought of her vow to "Aquerò", had taken advantage of her moment of freedom and had rushed off to Massabielle where she found fifty or so people already gathered. Nothing happened. As soon as she finished reciting her rosary, she started back full of anguish, wondering where she had failed. She decided to seek help from her confessor, Father Pomian, in whom she had confided from the outset of the visions. He observed that the authorities had no right to prevent her from going to the grotto. In fact, just about the same time, the very same "authorities" modified their rigid positions, due to the efforts of the mayor of Lourdes, M. Lacadé, who did not want to go against the evergrowing ranks of the citizenry following Bernadette. By Thursday it was no trouble to get permission to go to Massabielle and a hundred people were waiting for her. The Lady immediately appeared and the onlookers watched Bernadette in ecstasy for an hour or so. Of this meeting, she would later reveal that she had been told a secret, but that it was "only for her".

The Eighth Apparition

Wednesday, February 24. In the presence of three hundred or so onlookers Bernadette repeated her usual gestures. Unlike the previous times, her ecstasy seemed to make her suffer and her face often bore a melancholy expression. At a certain point, she crawled inside the grotto, bent over, nodded, started crying, then smiling, and finally kissed the ground. The onlookers' curiosity was aroused and they begged Bernadette to reveal her experience. "Penitence", the Lady had said, "Pray for the conversion of sinners". The Lady herself had requested that she kiss the ground ("if it wouldn't bother you") in penitence for sinners.

The Ninth Apparition

Thursday, February 25. At five o'clock in the morning , Bernadette, in the company of her aunts, was already at Massabielle. Despite the

as soon as he read a few lines, there were some mistakes so I said to him 'Sir, I never said that.' He got very angry and insisted that I had, while I kept repeating I hadn't".

The commissioner made a special point of Bernadette's not going to Massabielle any more. All the townspeople were excited and even though some believed and some didn't, this thing had to be stopped.

But Bernadette had already given her word, and nothing would make her go back on it, even the threat of prison was unable to shake her Nevertheless, the promise Jacomet failed to extract from Bernadette was made by her father — it mustn't have been very hard to cajole poor M.

Soubirous. Then, fearing the reaction of the excited crowd outside his door, Jacomet told Bernadette she could go.

The Seventh Apparition

Tuesday, February 23. The day before Bernadette had failed to convince her parents to let her go to the grotto and when she did go no encounter had taken place.

Obediently she had gone to school in the morning. After lunch she made another attempt to obtain her parents' consent, but they would not give it. In fact, to avoid surprises, Mme. Soubirous actually decided to accompany her daughter, who also

Internal view of the **Cachot**.

The Virgin of the Concession. ▶

The Grotto of Massabielle. (Reconstruction by Musée du «Petit Lourdes»).

rainy weather hundreds of onlookers, some pro, others con, were on hand at her arrival. She began to recite the rosary and soon fell into ecstasy. Suddenly she dropped the candle she was carrying and rushed inside the grotto where she bent down and kissed the ground. The she retraced her steps, but suddenly, as if she had been summoned, she ran back into the grotto, heading for the far left side. She appeared to be looking for something. In Bernadette's words "(the Lady) told me to go and cleanse myself in the spring. I saw none and went to the Gave. She replied that it wasn't there, and pointed at a spot below the precipice. I found a bit of water which looked more like mud, but there was so little I could hardly get any into my hand. I started digging and so I got more. It

was so salty that I had to spit it out three times".

The crowd watching all of these movements, grew more and more puzzled. The anti-Bernadettes had no doubts — she was evidently crazy. Questioned later, she replied that she didn't have the faintest idea why she had done what she had but that she had done what the Lady had asked of her and that was enough for her.

Another surprise was in store for her that day. Going against the mayor's wishes, Commissioner Jacomet, who was afraid of things getting out hand, had requested and obtained the intervention of the Imperial Procurator, M. Dutour. Bernadette was given a summons to appear before him. The same scene was repeated, M. Dutour exploiting every trick of his trade to make Ber-

nadette contradict herself. As she later recounted, "I told him the whole story which he put down in writing. Then he read the statement aloud ... he had added things I'd never said. So I told him, 'Sir, I never said such a thing".

The questioning went on for hours until M. Dutour, like Jacomet before him, was forced by the angry crowd outside to release Bernadette.

The Tenth Apparition

Saturday, February 27. As had happened after the Jacomet interrogation, the Lady failed to appear on Friday (Bernadette had gone despite M. Dutour's explicitly prohibiting her from doing so.)

On Saturday she returned to Massabielle and found an even greater crowd — according to M. Clarens, principal of the Lourdes High School, about 800 people were assembled. After having recited only a few Ave Marias, she fell into ecstasy, at which time she drank from the spring and went through the usual gestures of penitence.

The Eleventh Apparition

Sunday, February 28. The crowds kept growing and growing. That Sunday about 1500 people gathered to watch Bernadette repeat the gesture of penitence that the Virgin asked her to perform. As soon as she came out of her ecstasy she went off to church to attend Mass. Just as the previous Sunday, a policeman was waiting at the exit to take her to M. Dutour's office for further questioning, this time in the presence of M. Ribes, a magistrate. Scoldings, warnings, threats all failed to dent Bernadette's unshakable self-control.

The Twelfth Apparition

Monday, March 1. The crowd gathered to see Bernadette, again numbering about 1500 people, made it hard for her to reach the spring when she was in ecstasy. During this apparition, a strange event, later popularly known as the "Benediction of the Rosary", took place.

A sick friend of Bernadette's had given her a rosary and begged her to use it during the ecstasy. Even though Bernadette had her own with

The Grotto of Massabielle.

her, she took out her friend's but then immediately put it back into her pocket. Her hand emerged with the other rosary which she held out towards the niche.

Later she explained that "Aquerò" had told her to use her usual rosary and to hold it up. But, at the sight of her upraised hand, the onlookers all started to imitate her, lifting their rosaries with the hope of obtaining the Virgin's blessing.

The Thirteenth Apparition

Tuesday, March 2. The thirteenth vision was one of the most important of the mystic events — if such events can even be classified. Bernadette reached the grotto already thronged with onlookers. The crowd noticed nothing unusual compared to the previous visions, even though Bernadette was visibly shaken when she emerged from her ecstasy. "Aquerò" had asked her to tell the priests "to come here in procession ... and to erect a chapel on this spot". Aside from her confessor, Bernadette had never spoken to a priest about the visions, and she was thus a bit taken aback with the idea.

After a great deal of hesitation, accompanied by her aunts, she went to speak to the parish priest, Abbé Peyramale. She told him about the Virgin's first request and, as she received a curt reprimand in reply, she forgot to mention the chapel. Though Peyramale had been informed right from the start of the apparitions by Bernadette's confessor who had been granted permission to do so from Bernadette herself, he had always kept out of the matter. He had forbidden the clergy to take part in the Massabielle "meetings" and was patiently waiting for the excitement to boil over. The only way to react to the girl's scandalous behavior was to show her to the door.

When Bernadette realized her forgetfulness, she hadn't the heart to go back and face Peyramale. Dominiquette Cazenave, one of the

The Lacadé Mill.

most fervent believers in the apparitions and sister of M. Soubirous' employer, came to her aid by setting a meeting with the parish clergy for that very evening. In addition to Father Peyramale, Fathers Pène and Serres, the parish vicars, and Father Pomian were there to hear Bernadette repeat the request for a chapel. Repressing his instinctive severity which, unleashed, would only lead to another fit of anger, Peyramale instead asked the name of the Lady. Bernadette answered, just as she had earlier that morning, that she didn't know. "You've got to ask her", he promptly responded.

The Fourteenth Apparition

Wednesday, March 3, Bernadette, together with her mother and faithful aunt Bernarde, left for the grotto at seven in the morning. She had to cross a sea of human bodies to reach her customary place; an estimate of three thousand people (there were even some wading in the Gave) was made that day. Despite her prolonged prayers, Bernadette was not awarded with an apparition. Tears flowing down her face, she searched her mind for the reasons that might have been responsible for "Aquerò's" not appearing. Finally, she got up, went back home and returned to the school that she attended each day. That afternoon, her uncle advised her to go back to the grotto. When she arrived, she found the Lady awaiting her. As soon as she fell into ecstasy she posed Father Peyramale's question; as we read in her memoirs: "when I was inside the grotto, after reciting the rosary, I asked her, on behalf of our parish priest, to tell me her name". A tender smile was all she got for an answer.

When this was reported to Peyramale, his reaction was skeptical. While he couldn't deny that the visions had reawakened religious fervor in Lourdes, the whole matter was a dangerous affair. He reiterated his order that Bernadette should stop going to meetings with a stranger who probably was only out to pull her leg. If she really wanted a chapel built, she would just have to identify herself and give some sort of sign, for example, make the rose arbor in the grotto bloom. That would certainly be tangible enough proof of her powers.

The Fifteenth Apparition

Thursday, March 4. This was to be the last of the fifteen meetings promised by the Lady. By that time word of the apparitions had spread all over France. Commissioner Jacomet, after having carried out a minute inspection of the grotto the day before and the morning of March 4, had stationed an impressive contingent of police on the spot. The crowd was an estimated 8-10 thousand.

After attending a mass for a deceased relative at 6:30 am, Bernadette started off for the grotto. Two gendarmes made a breach in the crowd so she could pass, though it wasn't easy to keep her cousin Jeanne Védère at her side as she had promised. At the third Ave Maria of the second set of ten, she fell into her ecstasy which went on for about an hour in the customary manner. The thrill-seekers who were awaiting some kind of clamorous gesture from the Lady were to be disappointed.

Bernadette received no special revelation and she too felt a bit a sadness come over her. She went back to her miserable home, the Cachot, where a crowd had formed. Many people were there just to make her business proposals. Nevertheless, she kept her poise, remaining calm and collected throughout. That afternoon she went back to Father Peyramale and told him she had once more asked the Lady to identify herself and make the roses bloom. Both requests had been answered with a smile, yet "Aquerò" had in-

Bernadette father's house, also known as Moulin Lacadé reconstructed at the Musée du Petit Lourdes (above). Below, a present view of the house and of its bare interior.

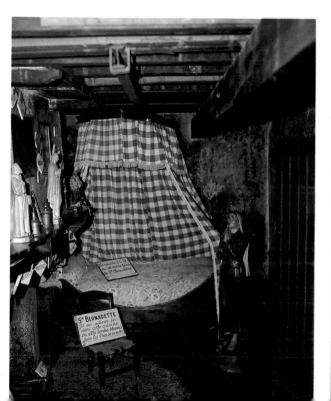

Bernadette Soubirous.

Thursday, March 25. Bernadette didn't sleep well — her Lady was calling. When she arrived at the grotto at 5:00 am, "Aquerò" was waiting for her. As soon as her rosary was said, she entered the grotto and when she returned her face was aglow with joy.

Dropping her candle in her great haste, she ran off to tell Peyramale the news. In her own words, Bernadette described the event: "... I again asked her who she was. Three times in a row I asked her. She continued to smile. Finally, I dared to ask one more time. She unclasped her hands and stood with her arms at her sides, then once more crossed her hands up to her breast, meanwhile looking up to heaven. And this was when she told me she was the Immaculate Conception...".

Peyramale asked her if she was certain of the Lady's reply. Bernadette said she was and that she had repeated the words — mysterious for her — the whole way back so she wouldn't forget them.

This day was the highpoint of the story of Lourdes. The definition "Immaculate Conception" was totally foreign to Bernadette's simple vocabulary — she at the time, was practically illiterate — and had to be explained to her later by M. Estradre: only the Virgin Mary could have said "I am the Immaculate Conception". Peyramale's doubts were dissipated. Even though his attitude would remain prudent and somewhat reserved, deep down he had already decided. He would later say that "even if the roses never bloomed, water undeniably did spout from the spring".

The Seventeenth Apparition

Wednesday, April 7. Although Bernadette had been drawn to the grotto during the past fortnight, the Soubirous had decided to be even more careful. On March 27 three doctors had been sent by the Prefect who was expecting them to commit Bernadette to a mental hospital — a Bernadette officially certified as mentally unbalanced would be very useful to him and his fellow public officials. But, although the doctors found nothing in Bernadette that would re-

sisted on the chapel. Peyramale was adamant — if she wanted the chapel she would have to say who she was and provide the funds to build it. At any rate, Bernadette herself felt tranquil, for she had fulfilled her promise and that was all she needed to be content.

At this point we must interrupt our story for a brief parenthesis. Bernadette's fifteen appointments were over. She continued the simple life she had always led. She spoke softly and coincisely when addressed and never went back to the grotto. She didn't know who she had encountered during her ectasies — she continued to speak of "Aquerò". She only knew that the vision was very beautiful. "She was so lovely", she reminisced many years later when it was already clear that "she" was the Virgin "that you can't wait to die so you can see her again".

All over France the matter was hotly debated. As always, public opinion was soon split into pros and cons. For every newspaper that denounced the triteness of the mystification, there was another that wrote glowing words emphasizing the poverty and lack of personal interest characterizing Bernadette and her family. And people continued to flock to the grotto to pray. On March 18 the authorities returned to question Bernadette. She would only confirm the facts, refusing to satisfy curiosity for curiosity's sake. Nor would she reveal her secrets which she declared "are only for me".

Nevertheless, she assured people that there was nothing terrible in her secrets and, from an investigative standpoint, the matter appeared to be closed.

Convent of St. Gildard at Nevers. Detail of St. Bernadette's face.

quire hospitalization, their embarassment led them to draft a rather ambiguous statement in which it was actually said that the "illness" Bernadette was suffering from "does not constitute danger to her health". It is clear that the Soubirous wanted to remain far from the public eye.

On April 7, for this very reason, the family was pretending that Bernadette was out of town. Nevertheless, when she reached the grotto at 5:00 am about a hundred people were already praying there. One of these was a scientist, Dr. Douzous, whom fate chose to record the "Miracle of the Candle", as it was later known. When she finished her rosary, Bernadette, as usual, crawled inside the grotto. She was holding a lit candle. Douzous could clearly observe that she was holding the flame beneath her left hand, apparently totally insensible. From habit as a man of science, he

scrupulously noted that Bernadette remained for a full fifteen minutes in that position. When the ecstasy was over, Douzous held her back a moment to examine her hand. There was absolutely no sign of a burn.

Three months passed during which Bernadette went about her life in the usual manner. Of course, people flocked to see her and question her, but she always acted in the same simple way. The poverty of her family remained unchanged, just as their living quarters, the gloomy Cachot. There were kind souls who would have liked to alleviate their misery, but Bernadette continued to refuse even the best-intentioned offers. Jacomet, on the other hand, was still lying in wait, ready to exploit any move of hers which could lend itself to misinterpretation. The events of Massabielle had caused an uproar. Visionaries were cropping up everywhere. In June M. Lacadé fenc-

ed off the grotto. Then, when the fence was immediately knocked down by the pilgrims, he had another one put up to replace it. The police prohibited visits to the grotto. Whoever was caught in the vicinity received a written notice that was then transmitted to court, the end result invariably being a trial ending in conviction. Actually, there were some excesses stemming from superstition, which the Bishop of Tarbes, Mons. Laurence, publicly denounced on July 11. Throughout the whole time Bernadette's behavior was detached and prudent. She advised others against going to the grotto and she herself didn't venture to the site.

On June 3 Bernadette took her First Communion in the Hospice chapel. Her joy was enormous. Finally, she had been able to make the dream she had held from the days of Bartrès come true.

The Eighteenth Apparition

Friday, July 16, the feast-day of the Virgin of Carmel. Even though Bernadette felt the call of the Virgin (whom she no longer called "Aquerò"), she was torn between her desire to heed it without telling anyone and her respect for authority, especially her family. She waited until night fell, and when it was dark (about 8 pm), accompanied by her aunt Lucile Castérot, she went down to Massabielle. To avoid curiosity seekers, she took the path along the right bank of the river. As soon as she began to recite the rosary before the grotto, the Virgin appeared. Thus, intermingled with the pilgrims and separated from the grotto by the waters of the Gave, Bernadette saw her Lady for the last time. When people later questioned how she could see from so far away, Bernadette replied, "I felt as if I were inside the grotto, just as close as the other times".

AT LOURDES AFTER THE VISION

Despite the extraordinary events she had lived through, Bernadette never changed. We might say that she picked up the threads of her old life, but she had never really dropped them. She continued to help with the housework and babysit to help her family. After her First Communion, she could no longer permit herself the luxury of continuing her schooling, though she did accept the aid of Mlle. Tardhivail so she could improve her French. The main difference was that she was always besieged — day after day — by every sort of visitor wanting to question her, often just out of plain curiosity. Many times the questions were full of traps, but Bernadette fended them off with great poise. She continued to thwart every attempt people made to give her money — "I want to remain poor", she flatly declared to a reporter who tried to convince her to go with him to Paris, dangling before her the mirage of vast riches. Likewise, she refused to touch devotional objects of any type.

In October 1858 the grotto closed by the prefect was reopened by personal order of Napoleon III, who was anxious to increase his popularity. In November Bernadette was examined by the Ecclesiastical Commission appointed by the Bishop of Tarbes. Bernadette's accounts were substantially all the same and her manner of reporting them was understated rather than dramatic. This kind of behavior never failed to leave a deep impression on those who came into contact with her.

At the beginning of 1860, Abbé Peyramale found himself facing some rather difficult problems. These included the ever-increasing — oft times indiscreet — visits, the attitude of the episcopacy which had not been officially made known even though there was good reason to think it would be favorable, and the financial straits of the Soubirous family — all of these problems had to be solved one way or another.

The problem of Bernadette's poverty was solved by a statagem. She was admitted to the Hospice run by the sisters of Nevers as an "indigent case", but the real purpose of sending her to a hospital was to get her out of the public eye and have her continue her education. On July 15 Bernadette left her family and moved into the Hospice. She rarely left the grounds. Her health worsened gradually but steadily, as her vocation grew stronger and stronger. In April 1862, one of her usual asthma attacks almost killed her, but in the meantime, on January 18, 1862, a pastoral letter issued by the Bishop of Tarbes declared that "the Immaculate Mary, Mother of God, really appeared to Bernadette" and that the apparition, "has all the characteristics of truth and the faithful have grounds for believing it certain". In April 1864 she finally manifested her desires. Forced to set aside her project of joining the Carmelite order on account of her poor health which would require "dispensation" from the rules, unacceptable to her, Bernadette chose to stay with the sisters who had welcomed her into their midst.

Nevertheless, only two years later in 1866, did she actually manage to enter the convent ranks, again due to her failing health. On July 3 she returned to the grotto for the last time and a day later she left Lourdes, never to return again.

THE LATER YEARS AT ST. GILDARD

Bernadette began her novitiate at the order's headquarters of St. Gildard at Nevers. During the ceremony of taking the veil, she received, as does every nun, a new name to symbolize her leaving the world: Bernadette would thereafter be known as Marie Bernard. From numerous eyewitness accounts, we know that she was exceedingly humble and modest, although the novices' head sister, fearful that her past experiences might turn her head, never failed to reprimand her for the slightest shortcoming. When the time came for her to take her temporary vows (October 30, 1867), for the same reason she was assigned to no specific task or destination. A good for nothing, as she herself was wont to say, she remained at St. Gildard helping out in the infirmary. Actually, this was another little stratagem conceived by the church authorities to keep her away from the ever present public curiosity and also to enable her to apply her gift for nursing which had already manifested itself when she was working in the Hospice of Lourdes.

Unfortunately, Sister Marie Bernard from nurse often turned patient. Three times it looked as if she would die from asthma and was given Extreme Unction. Then, by the time she pronounced her final vows on September 22, 1878, bone cancer of the knee had already been diagnosed and her time on earth was running out. After having carried out the mission of faith expressed by the apparitions, she felt the mission of suffering taking its toll of her body. On Wednesday, April 16, 1879, just after 3:00 pm, Sister Marie Bernard, a Crucifix tightly clasped to her breast, left this life.

THE SANCTUARIES

The Virgin had said to Bernadette, "Prayer and penitence — may pilgrims come here in great numbers." Her wish has been fulfilled. Lourdes is a place of continuous prayer and uninterrupted pilgrimage. In the Grotto, the atmosphere of peace and prayer that seeps into the hearts of the ailing and fit alike is conducive to the spiritual healing of each and every pilgrim whose spiritual communion with his fellows is total, whatever their homeland or skincolor.

This oasis of meditation, so far from the hustle and bustle of everyday life, is known as the "Dominion of the Grotto." Actually, it covers the areas which Bernadette referred to as "Massabielle", (dialect for Massa Vielle, i.e. the old cliff) and the Isle of Chalet. Bought by the Bishop of Tarbes in 1861 when official recognition of the visions appeared forthcoming, it has since undergone extensive changes. The waterway which once supplied the Savy Mill

has been filled in so that the Isle of Chalet is now joined to the rocky spurs, and the course of the Gave River has been deviated 40 meters northwards so that there would be more room around the Grotto. Yet, despite these changes, the environment of Bernadette's day has been preserved and safeguarded by isolating the area from the nearby city.

On this spot, where the Virgin had asked for a chapel, stands one of the greatest sanctuaries in the world. Three basilicas, one dedicated to the Immaculate Conception, one to the Rosary, and one to St. Pius X, put up in the course of the years, mark the development of devotion to the sanctuary.

The Breton Calvary. This moving sculpture carved from Finisters granite by Hernot, was a gift of the people of Breton to the Basilica of Lourdes. The statues at the corners represent the Virgin, St. Mary Magdalene, St. John, and St. Longinus who struck the Crucified Christ with his spear.

The Crowned Virgin. This outdoor statue, ▶ continuously adorned with bouquets of flowers left by the pilgrims ever since it was sculpted in 1877, faces the majestic basilicas of Lourdes.

THE BASILICA OF THE ROSARY

In few churches anywhere do architectural forms represent man's spiritual thrust towards God as they do, here. The Gothic-style towers soar upward as if to carry the hearts of the earthbound into the reaches of heaven, while the curving entrance ramps seemingly gather the pilgrims, bodies and souls, inside their gentle welcoming embrace.

The architect Hardy, who started work on the building in 1883, chose a design that would stylistically harmonize with the pre-existing upper basilica. His Romanesque-style domed building with a Greek cross plan is connected to the upper basilica by a double ramp which also acts as a frame for the façade.

The towers on either side of the dome were added on in 1908, the fiftieth anniversary of Bernadette's visions. The Basilica was opened in 1889, although it wasn't until October 6, 1901 that Cardinal Langénieux performed the solemn ceremony marking its official consecration.

21

The Esplanade. The open space before the basilicas.

Crowd of pilgrims attending the High Mass celebrated on the churchyard before the Basilica of the Rosary.

Pilgrims from every land flock to Lourdes, in what can only be described as an uninterrupted procession that has been going on for the last one hundred odd years. The never-ending stream is made up of both believers who have come to place themselves in the hands of the Virgin and non-believers who are invariably moved by the scenes of brotherly love that are enacted before their eyes.

Numerous prayers are recited during the impressive religious services held here. Yet what stands out most is not the grandiosity or number of participants, but rather the spirit of equality

The Eucharistic blessing of the sick, although different each time it is performed, is always pervaded by a feeling of genuine rejoicing.

The celebrant with the monstrance passing among the sick.

and the feeling of communion which pervades the whole.

The chalet meadow, the present-day Esplanade, with the churchyard of the Basilica of the Rosary as a backdrop, is often the scene of healings of the spirit as well as of the body. At 4:30 pm daily a procession starting from the Grotto carries the Holy Sacrament to the Esplanade. Fit and ailing march before the canopy under which a priest bears the monstrance. The procession symbolizes the march of man, together with Christ, toward God. When the canopy reaches the yard, the blessing of the sick begins.

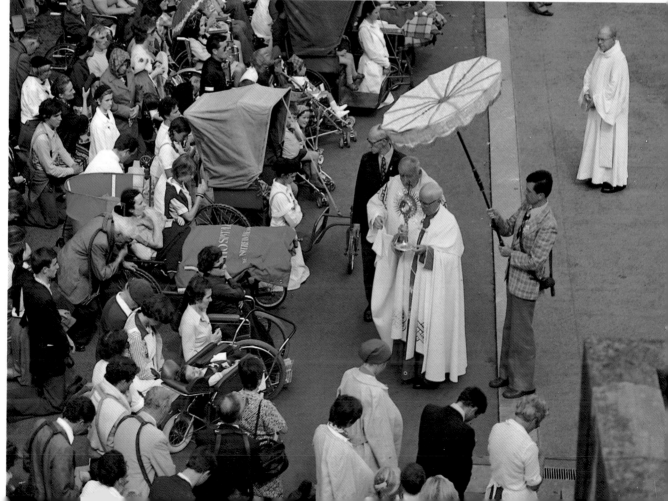

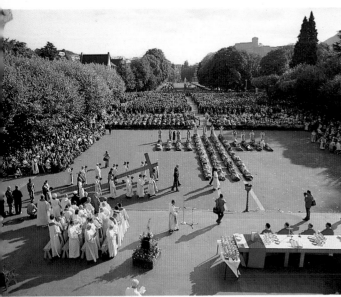

The Esplanade filled with pilgrims is one of the images of lasting memory when Lourdes is far away.

In addition to the High Masses and services generally held throughout the week, there are special services for pilgrimages organized by local church groups, dioceses, and associations. Pilgrims often witness moving rites that nevertheless differ from those they are accustomed to.

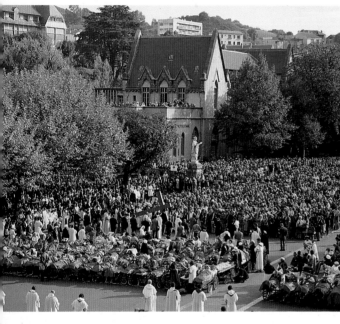

The Chapel of St. Pasquale Baylon.
Next to the altar of St. Bernadette is an altar dedicated to the protector of the Eucharistic works.

The Chapel of St. Bernadette, Beneath the lefthand staircase outside the Basilica of the Rosary, an altar to the Saint of Lourdes was erected in 1922. The statue is by Firmin Michelet.

INTERIOR OF THE BASILICA
OF THE ROSARY

Four of the Rosary chapels ▶

The huge hall, which can hold up to 2,500 people, is decorated in the Byzantine style. Daylight enters from windows cut into the bronze dome.

The apse's semi-dome is adorned with a fine mosaic of the Virgin surrounded by angels.

Inside the four arms of the Greek cross are fifteen chapels dedicated to the Mysteries of the Rosary.

The chapels celebrating the Mysteries of the Rosary are arranged radially about the transept and apse.

The elaborate mosaics adorning all but one are by the French artist, Facchina. The decoration of the Chapel of the Descent of the Holy Spirit, on the other hand, was executed by Venetian artists.

The devotion of the Rosary consists of 150 Ave Marias in groups of ten. Each series refers to meditation on a mystery of the life of Christ or the Virgin.

The mysteries are arranged in three groups: joy is the call of the worshipper to Faith, sorrow for meditation on Charity, and glory to nuture Hope.

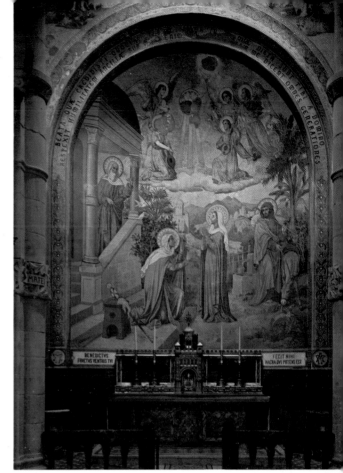

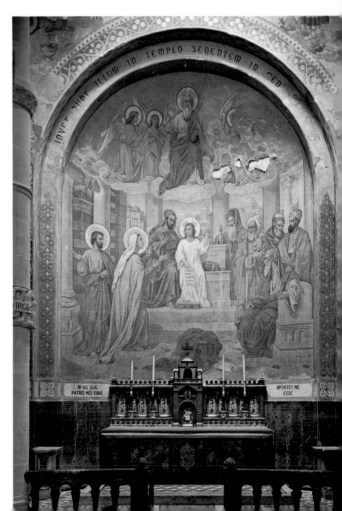

The main altar of the Crypt. The crypt contains five chapels. The middle one is dedicated to the Virgin Mother and there are always two nuns praying here.

The Virgin and Child.

◀ **Four of the Rosary chapels**

THE CRYPT

The crypt was the first place of worship to be built over the Grotto of the Apparitions. Begun at the same time as the upper basilica, it was finished in 1866.

The chapel was inaugurated the same year, on May 19, by the celebration of a High Mass.

Bernadette attended this service as well as the mass performed two days later in front of the Grotto, but she was mixed in with the Daughters of Mary to protect her from the crowds' curiosity. Serving as a place for prayer and meditation, the crypt lies beneath the apse of the Basilica of the Immaculate Conception and was built upon leveled solid rock.

THE BASILICA OF THE IMMACULATE CONCEPTION

The upper basilica dedicated to the Immaculate Conception stands on a cliff. 20 meters above the level of the River Gave. It was designed by Ippolito Durand in the neo-Gothic style. Begun in 1862, it took eight years to build.

When the crypt was inaugurated in 1866, Bernadette — who was to leave Lourdes immediately afterwards — could only see the supporting walls and where the pillars sustaining the nave would rise.

Although it was opened to the cult on August 15, 1871, the official consecration ceremony was not held until 1876 (July 1, 2, 3). 100,000 pilgrims were present at the services performed by 35 bishops and 3000 priests.

In 1874 Pope Pius IX bestowed the title of « Basilica Minor » on the church.

The façade of the Basilica of the Immaculate Conception dominated by the belltower's octagonal spire. A flower garland and gilded cross adorn the top of the tower, 90 meters above the level of the Gave.

The Basilica of the Immaculate Conception's stained glass windows. Each of the two rows of windows is a separate narrative cycle. The subject of the lower ones is the story of the Virgin of Lourdes; the upper ones recount the mystery of the Immaculate Conception.

THE GROTTO

The Grotto, Bernadette's Heaven, as the saint herself oft times referred to it, is the most mystic spot in all of Lourdes. A sense of spirituality pervades as nowhere else, for it was here that Bernadette felt the tremulous breeze announcing the apparition of the Virgin, and here, rapt in prayer, she had her holy visions.

From the very beginning, just weeks after the visions, water from the spring was channeled and collected in rudimentary tanks. Then, when work on the Basilica was begun and all the rubble was cleared from the Grotto, the exact spot where the water flows out of the rock was discovered.

When further work was carried out in 1948, at approximately two meters deep, it was found that there are two, not one, sources. The water is collected in two tanks named for the Rosary and the Isle of Chalet. From these tanks, it is piped into the pools and fountains.

The entrance to the Basilica of the Immaculate Conception.

The spring, protected by glass, spouts from the living rock.

The statue of the Virgin in white marble from Carrara placed in the ravine where the visions took place is by Joseph Fabish who was guided by indications given by Bernadette herself. The statue was donated by two sisters from Lyon who visited Lourdes in July 1863 and proposed placing a statue "resembling the Virgin as closely as possible" inside the Grotto. Bernadette, however, never cared for it — for, although she admitted that the statue was quite lovely, it just did not look like Her "(It was) too tall," she said, "and lacked Her smile and youthful appearance." Actually, due to a series of misunderstandings, Fabisch had failed to take into account certain observations that Bernadette had made before a photo of the model of the sculpture. In 1916 the words used by the Virgin to announce Herself ("Que soy era Immaculada Councepciou") were carved on the base. They are in the Patois dialect, the only language Bernadette knew at the time of the apparitions.

The statue was unveiled on April 4, 1864 before a crowd of 200,000.

Adoration of the sick in the Grotto

This is one of the ceremonies regularly held in Lourdes. In front of the Grotto, the pilgrims line up along the river so they can follow the rite deep in meditation. Thousands of candles, far too many even for the oversize candle holder placed in the Grotto, flicker from their special containers along the way.

Pilgrims from all over the globe come to offer the testimony of penitence requested by the Virgin.

THE FOUNTAINS

On February 25, the day of the 9th vision, the Virgin told Bernadette to enter the Grotto and drink the water that would spout from it. Bernadette did as she was told.

The water, which from muddy turned progressively clearer and clearer, gave rise to the ever-renewing miracle of the blessed thaumaturgical waters of Lourdes. Many theories have been advanced and many analyses performed for the purpose of scientifically discovering what makes the water so special. These scientific studies have revealed nothing that would warrant considering it anything but "ordinary water." Yet the scientifically-unexplicable healings are a fact. The rite of drinking and bathing in the water is widely practiced.

THE POOLS

The large capacity blue marble pools were built in 1955 to replace smaller ones closer to the Grotto, built in 1891 (moving them meant more space available around the Grotto itself). The penitential rite of bathing in the spring waters that the Virgin imparted to Bernadette was immediately widely imitated.

The first Church-certified miracle occured while the visions were still in act. Catherine Latapie, a farmgirl from a village in the vicinity of Lourdes, who had lost the use of the fingers on her right hand in a fall, arrived at the Grotto on March 1. She immersed her hand in the spring water when the vision was over. Immediately, a lovely warmth spread through her body and she was able to move her fingers again.

Before being announced by the Bishop, the authenticity of a healing must be certified by the Bureau Medical de Lourdes.

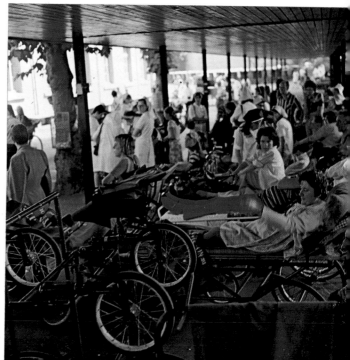

The "aux flambeaux" procession

This is undoubtedly the most moving ceremony held in Lourdes. Every evening, the candle-lit procession winds its way from the Grotto, down the Esplanade, to the church-yard of the Rosary. The procession is accompanied by chants of the Credo or Salve Regina from the pilgrims, each of whom carries a candle. The flickering lights symbolize the believer's desire to be in harmony with Christ "the light of the world."

THE BASILICA OF ST. PIUS X

This underground basilica was especially designed to accommodate the ever-growing crowds who, from every corner of the globe, come to regenerate themselves with love and hope.

Located to the left of the Esplanade, the church is a single hall of huge dimensions (81 × 201 meters) with a capacity of over 25,000 people. All the impressive ceremonies usually held before the Basilica of the Rosary may be held indoors here should there be inclement weather. Designed by Pierre Vago, André La Donné, and Pierre Pinsard, the poured concrete structure was built according to the most uptodate techniques between 1956 and 1968. Twenty-nine bays resting on hairpin pillars ten meters from the ground create a remarkable foreshortened effect.

The basilica was officially inaugurated on March 25, 1958 — the hundredth anniversay of the visions — by then Cardinal Angelo Roncalli, who, at the end of the same year, would become Pope John XXIII.

The Basilica of St. Pius X: Pax Christi Chapel. Along the ambulatory in the center of the hall is this chapel in which the Holy Sacrament is kept. ▶

The underground Basilica of St. Pius X.

The Accueil Notre-Dame. The hospital of Notre Dame rises inside the Domaine de la Grotte, its back to the Gave. Built in 1877 and enlarged several times afterward, it can accommodate up to 700 people.

The Accueil St. Bernadette. The new hospital was put up in the mid 1970s for the overflow from the Accueil Notre-Dame, as the old hospital was unable to handle the ever-growing crowds of pilgrims flocking to Lourdes.

Inaugurated in 1988, the **New Sanctuary of Lourdes** was designed by Architects J. P. Felix, C. Despre, J. P. Guinard e D. Yvon.
Its interior can accomodate up to 5,000.
In addition to the worship hall, various conference and meeting rooms can be found, accomodating up to 400.
Characterized by a sober, essential modern architecture, it is 100 m long and 80 m wide.

Via Crucis

The Via Crucis, inaugurated in September 1912, winds a kilometer and a half through the luxuriant vegetation of the Espelugues Hill. The over six-foot-high cast iron sculpture groups at each of the fourteen stations are by Raffle.

The **Holy Stairs** preceding the first station, symbolizing those Jesus climbed to reach the Pretorium of Pilate.

1st Station: Jesus is sentenced to die.

2nd Station: Jesus lifts the Cross.

3rd Station: Jesus falls the first time.

4th Station: Jesus encounters His Mother.

5th Station: Jesus is aided by Cyrenius.

6th Station: Jesus' face is wiped by Veronica.

7th Station: Jesus falls the second time.

8th Station: Jesus speaks with the women.

9th Station: Jesus falls the third time.

10th Station: Jesus is unclothed.

11th Station: Jesus is crucified.

12th Station: Jesus dies on the Cross.

13th Station: Jesus removed from the Cross.

14th Station: Jesus is placed in the tomb.

15th Station: Resurrection.

56

JOHN PAUL II
A PILGRIM
AT LOURDES

14-15 August 1983

"I have become a pilgrim together with you. I shall live with you, in a very simple way, a typical day of pilgrimage, through gestures and demonstrations of compassion which here, every day, show their evangelical and ecclesiastical authenticity as well as their spiritual fertility. I strongly wished to make this pilgrimage. God has answered my prayers today by allowing me to be amongst you. Blessed be God! Yes, blessed be God: the Father, the Son and the Holy Ghost, for having prepared here for Bigorre, the Pyrenees, France and for the whole Church, such a place of prayer, recollection, faith and reconciliation".

"Dear sick in health, I wish to leave in your memories and hearts three small lights which I believe to be precious: may you be clearly aware of your suffering without minimizing or exaggerating it... Accept it, not through resignation, but because our faith assures us that the Lord can and wants to bring good out of bad... The most beautiful gesture is that of oblation, the offering made for the love of the Lord and our brothers".

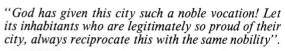

"God has given this city such a noble vocation! Let its inhabitants who are legitimately so proud of their city, always reciprocate this with the same nobility".

"Let us keep vigil this peaceful night. Let us keep vigil whilst we wait to celebrate the Glory of Mary. Let us pray. Let our prayers unite and rise towards God like the flames of our candles, to offer Him, together with Mary, a fervent act of thanks...".

"*Oh Mother of Christ, you who stand at the foot of your Son's Cross, be close to all those who are persecuted in the world of today! Let your maternal presence help them to bear their sufferings and to bring back victory through the Cross!*".

THE TOWN OF LOURDES

The Castle

by Jean Robert, Curator of the Pyrenees Museum.

Strategically perched on an isolated cliff in the middle of the Valley of the Gave du Pau, the old feudal castle was now and then the residence of the Counts of Bigorre during the 11th and 12th centuries.

Under the Treaty of Bretigny (1360), it was given over to the English. Later Prince Nero appointed Pierre-Arnaud and Jean de Béarn to command it. Leading a group of Gascon mercenaries under the protection of Gaston Fébus, they repeatedly sacked the county until its fall in 1407. Besieged several times in the Middle Ages, at the end of the reign of Louis XIV the castle was turned into a state prison. The building was remodeled many times throughout the centuries and was practically entirely rebuilt between 1820 and 1880 by the Army Engineering Corps. Nevertheless, it has retained the rectangular, approximately 24 meter tall donjon topped by machicolation and today occupied by the Pyrenees Museum. Declassed by the French army in 1889, it was purchased by city of Lourdes in 1894.

The Parish Church

Dedicated to the Sacre Coeur, this church took many years to put up. Although it was begun by Father Peyramale in 1875, work went on at snail's

pace on account of the financial straits of the Lourdes parishes, and it could only be officially inaugurated in 1903.

The belltower was finished in 1936. The Romanesque parish church of Saint Pierre, almost a thousand years old, where St. Bernadette prayed, was destroyed in 1904. It was located a bit to the west, on the site of the present-day Place Peyramale. The oldest fittings, and those connected with Saint Bernadette, have been transferred to the new church where, in the crypt, lie the mortal remains of Father Peyramale.

Pic du Jer. A pleasant 12 minute rackrail ride takes you up to the Pic du Jer (948 meters above sealevel). There is a breathtaking view of Lourdes spread out below.

◀ The **Baptismal font.** This Romanesque granite font was where Bernadette Soubirous was christened on January 9, 1844.

The Wax Museum

Opened to the public on July 1, 1974, the Wax Museum has encountered great success. It is the only wax museum in the world dealing exclusively with a religious subject. It was set up as a joint project in conjunction with the Musée Grévin in Paris which supplies the wax figures. The lifesize — and incredibly lifelike — figures are placed in splendid *son et lumière* settings.

The museum's over 800 square yards of exhibition space are laid out on five floors (elevators are provided for the handicapped). There are 125 wax figures. The first floor exhibits recount the life of Bernadette Soubirous, the upper floor exhibits the life of Christ. One of the highlights is an exact reproduction of Leonardo's Last Supper.

The modelling of wax figures predates Antiquity and was known to both the Egyptians and Greeks. In the 16th century the custom of portraying well-known contemporary figures became widespread — this was the origin of the 18th century wax museum. Later Alfred Grévin, a French satirist who lived in the 19th century, revived the wax museum idea in 1882 by founding the Grévin Museum in Paris, the world's most celebrated wax museum, and closely connected to the Lourdes Museum.

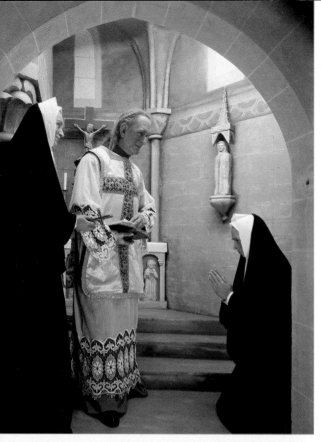

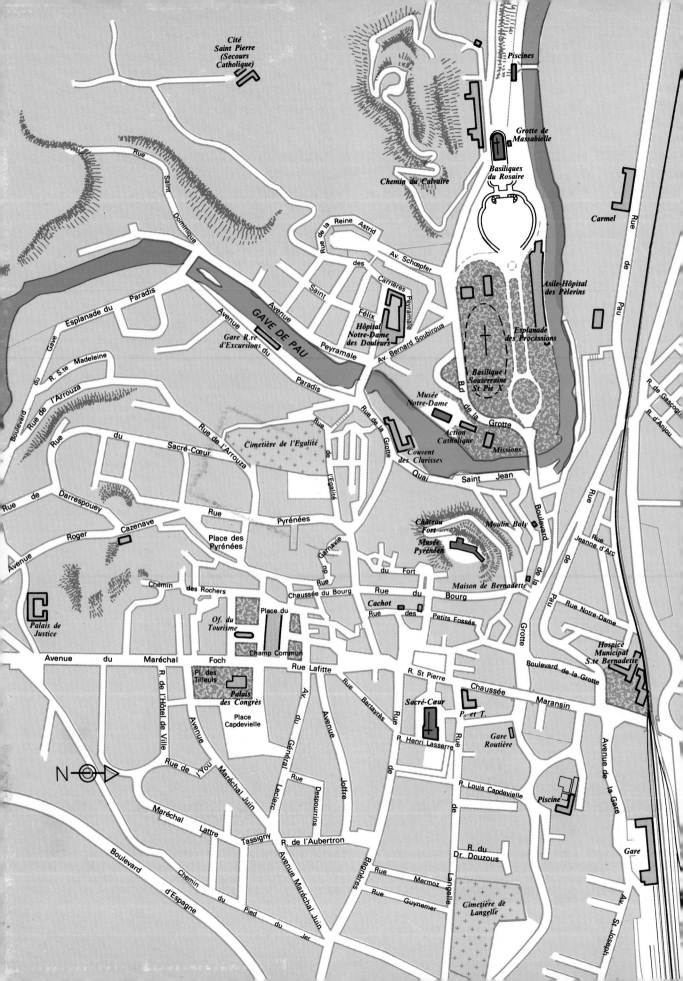